FLYING THE
SPACE SHUTTLES

FLYING THE SPACE SHUTTLES

Don Dwiggins

ILLUSTRATED WITH PHOTOGRAPHS

DODD, MEAD & COMPANY
New York

Frontispiece: Cutaway view of a Space Shuttle.

PICTURE CREDITS

National Aeronautics and Space Administration, 2, 14, 15, 16, 17, 25, 26, 29, 31, 35, 40, 42–43, 45, 46, 47, 53, 54, 55, 56, 57; Rockwell International, 12, 19, 21, 22, 23, 33, 34, 36, 37, 38, 41, 49, 51.

First published, 1985, in the United States
by Dodd, Mead & Company, New York
All rights reserved under International and
Pan-American Copyright Conventions
No part of this book may be reproduced in any form
without permission in writing from the publisher
Distributed in Canada by
McClelland and Stewart Limited, Toronto
Printed in Hong Kong by South China Printing Company

Library of Congress Cataloging in Publication Data
Dwiggins, Don.
Flying the space shuttles.
Includes index.
Summary: Describes the history and uses of the
space shuttle, how it works, and the details of
typical flight.
1. Space shuttles—Juvenile literature.
[1. Space shuttles]   I. Title.
TL795.5.D95   1985   629.45′4   84-23898
ISBN 0-396-08510-5

This book is dedicated to America's courageous men and women astronauts who have made the dream of living in space come true.

The author wishes to thank his many friends in aerospace who assisted in compiling this record of America's conquest of space in this age of Space Shuttles and coming Space Stations. Special thanks go to Donald L. Zylstra, Chief of NASA's Publications & Support Services Branch; Ralph Jackson at NASA/ Dryden Flight Research Center; and Sue Cometa of Rockwell International's Space Transportation & Systems Group.

Contents

Foreword

When I was a boy, we used to play with model airplanes and dream that they would fly way beyond the Earth, perhaps even to the Moon. Well, in 1969, we did get to the Moon, but not in an airplane. We got there in a capsule, launched by a huge rocket.

Today we are flying into space routinely, in a ship that looks like an airplane, but there is a big difference. The ship is launched like a rocket, flies in space like a spaceplane, and comes back to Earth to land like an airplane.

It is called the Space Shuttle. And it has given us a new look at our world and the means to do many new things in space. The Space Shuttle is leading us to the next giant step—a permanently occupied Space Station, where today's boys and girls may one day live and work to make life better for us all.

To young people today, going into space is no longer a dream. It is a great adventure that can be realized if you work hard and seek a career in science and technology. Future astronauts will help shape our new frontier as a place for peace and doing useful things for everybody on Earth. I hope that all of you who are reading this book will someday join them.

JOHN M. BEGGS
ADMINISTRATOR
National Aeronautics and
Space Administration

Introduction

After a quarter-century of exploring space with small, one-man, two-man, and three-man space capsules, today's astronauts flying Space Shuttles are finally opening the way to live permanently in space.

Space Shuttles arc huge, delta-winged aerospace craft, big as airliners. Men and women astronauts and scientists ride them into Earth orbits, to perform all sorts of experiments in weightlessness. Instead of the cramped quarters of those earlier space capsules and having to wear heavy pressurized space suits for the entire trip, they work in comfortable flight suits. Once in orbit, there are bunk beds, menus with a wide variety of foods, living arrangements as convenient as possible in weightlessness.

The trips begin with the thunder and fire of a rocket launch, and after spending days or weeks in almost circular orbits, Space Shuttles return to Earth through the atmosphere like big gliders.

Space Shuttles are really space cargo ships that carry satellites and other scientific payloads, along with their flight crews and technicians. Some pick up other satellites and repair them, or bring them back to Earth for a major overhaul. In the future they will serve as shuttle links between Earth and orbiting Space Stations.

Space Shuttles can be flown over and over for as many as 100 trips. Because the Orbiter is reusable and the two rocket boosters are recoverable, they save millions of dollars in launch costs. Only the giant external fuel tank is lost. Space Shuttles form the heart of the Space Transportation System (STS).

CHAPTER 1

Let's Take a Trip into Space

Flying in a Space Shuttle is much like flying in a big airliner. The main difference is weightlessness, and at takeoff you "blast off" straight up from the launch pad, atop a storm of fire and smoke. You're strapped in your seat lying head down, but wearing a comfortable flight suit, not a pressurized space suit. A helmet and removable communications headgear complete the outfit.

Solid rocket boosters attached to the external fuel tank are largest ever flown. Each 150 feet tall, they deliver 5,200,000 pounds of thrust.

As your Shuttle rises faster and faster, it picks up speed smoothly, so the gravity load increases only to 3 g and your body weight increases only three times. If you weigh 100 pounds on Earth, for a brief moment you'll weigh 300 pounds. (A "g" is the force or pull of Earth's gravity on your body at sea level. On some earlier manned space flights, the g load went as high as 8.1 g.) Your heart may beat faster for a while, until the excitement of the launch passes. Then you can relax and look out the window at the Earth, hundreds of miles below.

Every 90 minutes in orbit you'll see a new sunrise

and sunset, and the cabin air you breathe is just like back on Earth. But you'll get a surprise when you start to move around. Instead of weighing 100 pounds or 300 pounds, you'll weigh nothing at all!

Riding in orbit at about 17,500 miles an hour, the pull of gravity is nearly balanced by what is called centrifugal force. The slight difference is called microgravity. You are in a condition of weightlessness. If you bend down to pick up something, you may end up doing somersaults. So you'll use portable handholds with suction cups.

Astronaut Thomas Mattingly prepares a meal on *Columbia*'s mid-deck, using scissors to open a plastic drink container.

Even eating is different in space. Your fork and spoon will drift off the table if you aren't careful. Crumbs will float upward, a danger if you inhale them. And spilled water doesn't drip down. It, too, floats up, in tiny balls that stick to the wall and spread like glue.

To make sure you eat well, there's a menu of more than 100 different kinds of food in the locker. Much of it is dehydrated. There are cereals, vegetables, eggs and fruit, steak and shrimp. There are 20 kinds of beverages, including tea and coffee, also dehydrated. But no pure orange juice or whole milk. When water is added to them, the orange crystals turn to "rocks" and milk floats around in lumps and tastes bad. But on a six-day flight, you can eat a different meal three times a day every day.

The Shuttle's galley has an oven, hot and cold water faucets, trays, silverware, wet and dry wipes. To fix a meal you take out the plastic-wrapped pouch marked for that day and meal—Day 2, Meal A. For dehydrated or freeze-dried items, you inject the correct amount of water through a hollow needle. Articles to be heated are placed in the oven. Food trays have magnets on them.

Astronauts Frederick Hauck, Norman Thagard, Sally Ride, and
John Fabian take time out from chores to prepare a meal snack.

LET'S TAKE A TRIP INTO SPACE

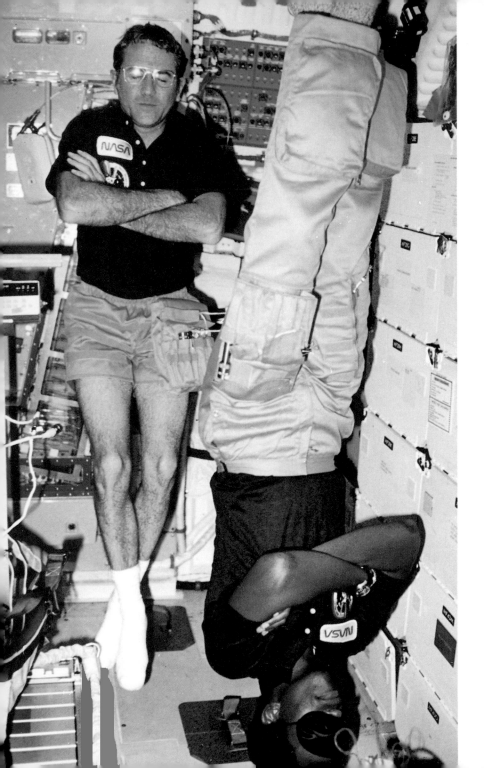

At the table you'll eat standing up, held in place by suction cups on your shoes. Table manners are important in space. Eat slowly and gracefully, with no sudden movements that could make your food float away. And take small bites.

After supper it's time to turn in for a good night's sleep. Across the mid-deck from the galley is a two-tier bunk. A third sleeper can stretch out underneath, and a fourth can sleep standing up. There's no sense of up or down in zero gravity. You could sleep standing on your head, for that matter.

Each bed is a padded board with a fireproof sleeping bag attached. After stowing your outer clothing, you crawl into your bag and zip it up, then fasten the straps around your waist. The hard board you sleep on feels soft as a comfortable mattress.

To stay healthy in space, you need exercise. Step on a small treadmill, adjust straps to your waist, and jog to music from a tape deck. Turn on an air duct to keep cool. If you don't, you'll need a vacuum

Commander Richard Truly (left) naps on his toes, while Mission Specialist Guion Bluford sleeps on his head in weightless comfort.

cleaner to remove the sweat from your skin. It sticks, like any water drops in zero gravity.

The Shuttle's water supply is a byproduct of fuel cell operation that makes electricity for the spacecraft. There are three fuel cells, each with 32 plates. When liquid oxygen is applied to one side of the plate, the liquid hydrogen to the other, each plate produces one volt of electricity, Pure water comes from combining oxygen and hydrogen to make H_2O at a rate of 15 pounds per hour, enough for the whole crew.

There are no showers on a Shuttle. Instead, you'll take a sponge bath. The water and liquid soap stick to your skin, so you wash with one cloth and use another to rinse yourself.

There is a curtained toilet with a seat belt to hold you on. The waste material is sucked by a fan into a compartment below deck, where it is dried and disinfected. Liquid wastes are pumped into a tank under the floor.

Your personal kit contains items such as extra clothing, toothbrush and toothpaste, a comb, a nail clipper. Your nails grow slowly in space, so you'll only need to trim them once a month.

One big problem is motion sickness, caused by weightlessness. More than 30 percent of Shuttle astronauts have suffered from it, with dizziness, nausea, cold sweats, headaches, and drowsiness. It lasts only about three days. Space doctors say it may be due to the difference between what your eyes and your inner ears tell the brain. In weightlessness, the semi-circular canals that provide orientation act differently than on Earth.

Astronaut Sally K. Ride talks to ground control from mid-deck of *Challenger*.

Long-duration Shuttle flights cause muscles and bones to deteriorate somewhat, and the heart to grow slightly smaller. This is due to the lack of a constant gravity stress in weightlessness. Exercising on the treadmill creates the resistance the body is accustomed to on Earth. Future Space Stations will need some sort of artificial gravity to keep people healthy.

But for normal Shuttle flights of a week to a month, biomedical data gathered over the years of manned space exploration tell us that the space environment is relatively safe.

When it's time to return to Earth, you'll strap yourself down again. But first you put on an inflatable pair of pants, called an anti-gravity suit, to prevent blacking out on the return from weightlessness to Earth gravity. The Shuttle commander will flip the craft around tailfirst and fire rockets to slow down from orbital velocity. Then he turns the Shuttle end-for-end again, to begin entry of the atmosphere at 400,000 feet and halfway around the world from where touchdown will take place.

Computers take over to set up a letdown procedure covering 4,000 miles. Air friction sets up an electrical blackout of all communications with the ground. Intense heat raises the temperature of the Shuttle's nose and leading edges to more than 3000° F. But protective thermal tiles keep the Shuttle safely cool.

After maneuvers to correct the flight path and speed, the Shuttle is lined up with tle landing site. The approach starts at about 14,000 feet altitude, with the speed at 333 miles per hour. The descent path is seven times as steep as that of a commercial airliner. There is no motor noise because the Shuttle lands like a glider, without engines. At about 1,750 feet, the nose is pulled up to slow down, and you land at something over 200 mph.

The commander or the autopilot makes the landing, so that the 100-ton craft touches down gently, to roll to a stop in perhaps 8,000 to 9,000 feet. It's been a perfect flight!

Space Shuttle *Challenger* flares out for landing, with NASA jet chase plane alongside.

CHAPTER 2

How the Shuttle Works

Today's Space Shuttle is the largest type of spacecraft Americans have flown into space. First was the one-man Mercury spacecraft. Alan Shepard reached an altitude of 166½ miles in it on May 5, 1961. On February 20, 1962, John Glenn was the first American in orbit when he flew three orbits in the Mercury capsule, *Friendship 7*.

Next came the two-man Gemini spacecraft, making orbital flights during 1965 and 1966. Gemini spacecraft could be steered in orbit to link up with other satellites.

Later, there was the three-man Apollo space cap-sule, designed to transport men to the Moon and back. In 1969, Neil Armstrong was the first man on the Moon. A part of the Apollo project was a space ferry called the Lunar Module, or LM. It took astronauts from the Apollo, which was in lunar orbit, to the Moon's surface and back.

In 1975, the Apollo linked up in space with Russia's two-man *Soyuz* spacecraft. The two crews visited each other through a tunnel. In 1973–74, Apollo was used to transport crews to the 100-ton orbiting spacecraft known as Skylab, big as a small house. Three astronaut crews visited Skylab, and lived in space for as long as three months. The crews brought back 300,000 photographs of the Sun, 40,000 pictures of Earth, and 230,000 feet of data on magnetic tape.

Today's Shuttle Orbiters are the first true aerospace craft. Huge, roomy, and comfortable to live in, they are 122 feet long and weigh 200,000 pounds. At lift-off, with their giant rocket boosters and external fuel tank, they weigh 4½ million pounds!

There are four aerospace craft in the Shuttle fleet— *Columbia, Challenger, Discovery,* and *Atlantis.* An earlier Shuttle, the *Enterprise,* was used as a test vehicle to train Shuttle crews to glide down through the atmosphere and land. It was carried piggyback to 24,100 feet atop a 747 jet plane for launching.

First Shuttle to go into orbit, the STS-1 *Columbia* was flown by Commander John W. Young and Pilot Robert L. Crippen. They traveled more than 1,000,000 miles in three orbits. Launched from Kennedy Space Center at Cape Canaveral in Florida on April 12, 1981, *Columbia* landed two days later on the dry lakebed at Edwards Air Force Base in California.

The mobile launch platform at Cape Canaveral was the same one used for Saturn V rockets that

Compared to a Space Shuttle, the Apollo space capsule that took men to the Moon was small and crowded.

sent Apollo astronauts to the Moon. The Space Shuttle launches travelers into an easterly orbit, to get an extra kick from the Earth's rotation.

It took only four Shuttle launches, STS-1 through STS-4, to thoroughly check out the system, with more than 1,100 special tests. Since then there have been a few "glitches," or minor malfunctions.

One "glitch" cancelled the launch of Space Shuttle *Discovery* early in 1984, just four seconds before lift-off. The computer controlling an engine valve was blamed. It was fortunate the abort system worked. Had the launch proceeded, loss of one of the three main engines would have meant ditching in the Atlantic Ocean and losing the Orbiter.

The three engines gulp liquid hydrogen and oxygen from the 154-foot-high external fuel tank, big as a small dirigible. In four seconds they build to 90 percent power. Then the two solid fuel rocket boosters fire, in a storm of fire and smoke, and the craft rises slowly and majestically toward space.

Left: Apollo space capsules took men to the Moon. This is Astronaut David Scott, with Lunar Module in background.

Right: Skylab was an orbiting laboratory, big as a small house.

After two minutes of flight, the two solid fuel rocket boosters are cut loose, to land by parachute in the ocean. They are recovered for reuse. Then, eight minutes into the flight, the Orbiter's three main engines shut down. The external tank is cast off, to break up on re-entry, the only part of the Shuttle that won't be used again.

The Orbiter, flying upside down, goes into orbit at 17,500 miles an hour, under thrust from two small maneuvering engines that burn for 105 seconds.

The acceleration forces are now gone, and your body weight, which climbed from a normal 100 pounds to 300 pounds, drops to almost nothing. It's time to relax and enjoy the incredible view of Earth from about 150 miles up.

The astronaut crew and mission specialists ride in the forward cabin. It is divided into a forward flight deck and mid-deck living space, with the cargo bay and engine compartment farther back. The upper flight deck looks like the cockpit of a DC-10 jetliner. The Shuttle commander sits at the left, the pilot on the right. Both face an instrument panel that has three TV-like cathode ray tube (CRT) displays of flight data. All critical Shuttle systems are in triplicate, as a safety precaution. Should one system fail, a second takes over. If that fails, the third is available.

There are two more positions on the flight deck for an astronaut mission specialist and a scientist in charge of the payload data. Other specialists will ride at mid-deck positions.

When the Orbiter must maneuver close to another spacecraft or satellite, the commander goes to the rendezvous and docking station. It faces aft on the left side of the flight deck. To his right is the payload handling station, where the pilot can remotely manipulate, deploy, release, or capture payloads.

As soon as the Orbiter is in orbit, the cargo bay doors are opened. The doors expose radiators that release heat from the Orbiter into space. With the doors closed, heat builds up inside. Along one side of the cargo bay is a 50-foot Remote Manipulator Arm, sometimes called a "space crane." Like your own arm, it has a movable shoulder joint, elbow, and wrist, and a four-claw hand at the end.

A TV camera on the "wrist" helps the pilot direct the arm to lift a satellite from the payload bay and release it into orbit. The arm can also capture an orbiting satellite and bring it aboard for repair, or to return it to Earth.

Living quarters aboard the Orbiter are in the mid-deck area, beneath the flight deck. Thirteen feet long, it tapers from 12 to 9 feet, looking forward. To your left is the private toilet, wash basin, and mirror, and also the galley. To your right are drawer-size lockers and bunk beds. More storage lockers line the forward wall space, some of them holding the food supply arranged by day and meal.

At the rear of the mid-deck is a ladder to reach the flight deck, and a large airlock, through which the specialists can crawl back into the 60-foot-long payload bay. Here is where the action is!

Flight deck of Orbiter *Columbia*. Note three CRT TV-like display tubes on panel with green flight information.

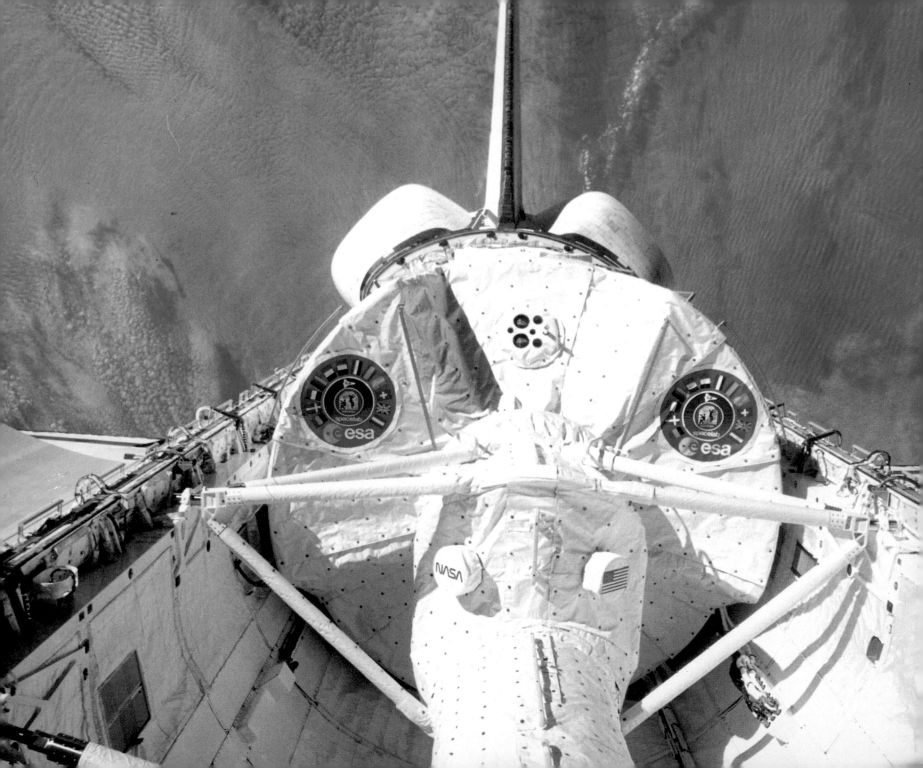

The Spacelab

Big as a school bus, the billion-dollar Spacelab made its first trip into space in the cargo bay of Space Shuttle *Columbia* on its flight in November, 1983.

The six-man crew was the largest ever flown in a Shuttle. (An eight-man crew is scheduled to fly in 1985.) Commander John W. Young was the world's most-experienced space traveler. He had spent 27 days in space, including three days living on the Moon. The pilot was Brewster H. Shaw, Jr., a former Air Force test pilot. Young and Shaw spent most of their time on the flight deck, shooting pictures out the window.

The four-man Spacelab crew, all PhDs, were Owen K. Garriott and Robert A. R. Parker, mission specialists, and Byron K. Lichtenberg and Ulf Merbold, payload specialists. Merbold, from West Germany, was the first non-American launched into space aboard an American spacecraft.

Spacelab was designed to NASA specifications, built, and financed by the European Space Agency

View of Spacelab in cargo bay of *Columbia*. Docking tunnel, in foreground, leads to Spacelab's shirt-sleeve environment.

(ESA), a group of ten nations, including Austria, Belgium, Denmark, France, West Germany, Italy, The Netherlands, Spain, Switzerland, and the United Kingdom.

Spacelab allows non-astronaut scientists to run their own experiments in a shirt-sleeve environment. It is built in two segments, each 9 feet long and 13 feet in diameter. Joined together, they form a compartment like the inside of a big passenger jet. Behind it in the cargo bay is a U-shaped pallet, 10 by 13 feet.

The pallet can hold three tons of instruments to study astronomy, space physics, and Earth sciences in the vacuum of outer space. Unlike the orbiting laboratory Skylab, which had an operational lifetime of only eight months, the Spacelab can be flown over and over. On its first flight, Spacelab carried 71 experiments.

To study the Sun and stars, the Orbiter flies right side up. To study the Earth, it flies upside down. One of the Shuttle's three fuel cells provides electrical power for Spacelab.

Spacelab scientists, working in two 12-hour shifts, study strange, electrified gases called plasmas that the Shuttle flies through. They can locate minerals on Earth and study pollution in the atmosphere. Working in weightlessness, they study ways to make new kinds of materials and medical products. In the future, this work will lead to space manufacturing in the zero gravity of tomorrow's huge Space Stations.

The scientists enter Spacelab through an aluminum tube $3\frac{1}{3}$ feet in diameter. Once inside, they work with all sorts of instruments on their various projects. The walls are lined with switches, cathode ray tube (CRT) screens, and racks filled with standard equipment, like they use on Earth. Overhead ceiling bins hold cameras, film, test tubes, lab cultures, spare parts, tools—everything they'll need for their work.

TV monitor in Spacelab is viewed by (left to right) Specialists Robert Parker, Byron Lichtenberg, Owen Garriott, and Ulf Merbold aboard *Columbia*.

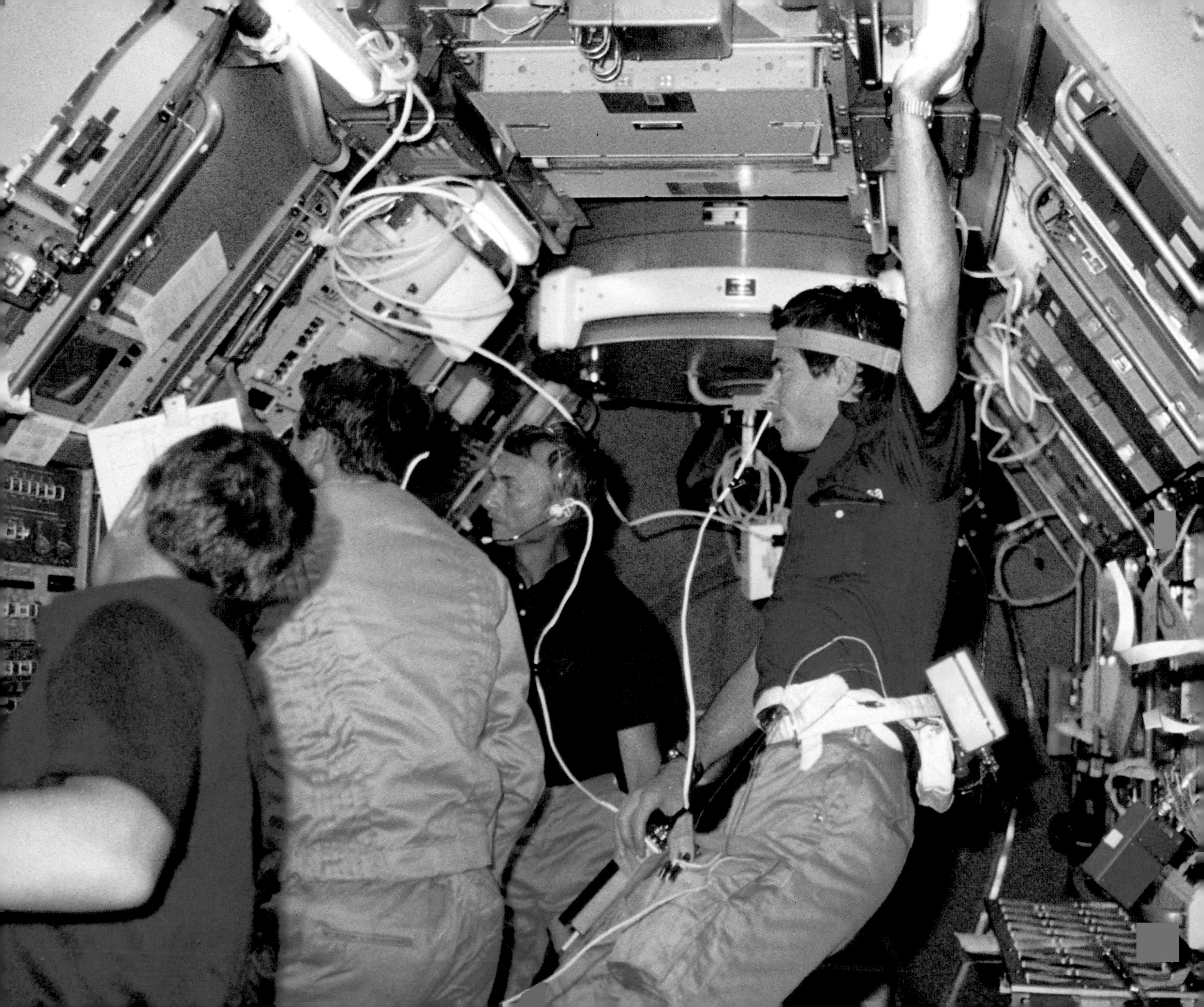

CHAPTER 4

It's a GAS

Do you have a very special experiment you'd like to try out aboard a Space Shuttle? NASA will be glad to help you. For a fee—$3000 to $10,000—you can have it carried into space. The flight crew will turn it on and off for you.

Such individual experiments are called Getaway Specials, or GAS for short. Hundreds of GAS experiments have already reserved space on Shuttle flights, including ones from high school students. GAS experiments do not have to be flown in the Spacelab. They can be carried on any Shuttle flight when there is room for them. All, of course, need NASA approval to get aboard.

The experiments have to be useful—to aid research or development. They must weigh less than 200 pounds, take up no more than 5 cubic feet, and require no services from Shuttle crews other than turning them on or off. This means that they must be self-contained, with their own power system, and whatever is needed for recording data.

On the Space Shuttle flight in February, 1984, *Challenger* carried five GAS experiments. They ranged from a soldering experiment to a study of seed germination. On the next Shuttle flight, a box full of bees was aboard in an experiment by student Dan Poskevich as part of the Shuttle Student Involvement Program. He wanted to find out if bees built their honeycombs in zero gravity the same way they do on Earth. The experiment showed that they could.

Earlier, aboard *Columbia* in 1982, two other student experiments studied the growth of a sponge called Porifera, and chemical crystals to find out if perfect crystals could grow in space.

The main goal of some on-board experiments is to find out if drugs such as insulin can be produced of far greater purity than on Earth. Success would help in fighting diseases.

Another important series of experiments is called the Continuous Flow Electrophoresis System (CFES). CFES was designed to separate biological materials, such as egg albumin, using their surface electrical charges in zero gravity. Such work will lead to manufacturing pure medical products in space.

Above: Astronaut James van Hoften examines beehive aboard *Challenger*. Space experiment was suggested to NASA by student Dan Poskevich.

Right: Astronaut Guion Bluford checks pump on Continuous Flow Electrophoresis System experiment in mid-deck area of *Challenger*.

31

CHAPTER 5

Walking in Space

There are times during a Space Shuttle flight when an astronaut must go outside to perform special jobs. At the back of the cabin, he opens the hatch of an airlock and enters. He closes the door and climbs into his space suit. It provides oxygen and suit cooling for six hours. A backpack in the upper part of the suit contains a miniature life-support system.

With flashlight and tools attached to the suit, he opens the airlock hatch to the outside, attaches a tether, and crawls into the cargo bay. The huge doors of the cargo bay area were opened from the flight deck shortly after the Shuttle reached orbit.

The area is open to space. He needs the flashlight because half of a three-hour stay will be spent on the dark side of Earth.

His job may be to take pictures of a payload, install or remove instruments, film, or materials for the payloads, set up antennas, examine the thermal tiles on the outside of the Orbiter, or perhaps repair some damaged or malfunctioning mechanism.

Such trips outside the Shuttle cabin are called EVAs—Extra-Vehicular Activities. Two crew members can go outside at the same time, each in his own space suit.

For space walks away from the Orbiter, astro-

Astronauts F. Story Musgrave (left) and Donald Peterson float in *Challenger's* cargo bay during EVA. Both have tethers attached to safety slide wires.

WALKING IN SPACE

Manned Maneuvering Unit (MMU) lets astronauts fly away from the Orbiter and return. You can be your own spaceship!

nauts wear newly developed MMUs—Manned Maneuvering Units. The MMU allows an astonaut to visit other orbiting spacecraft. It's like a flying armchair that attaches to the space suit's backpack.

The MMU is propelled in space by two dozen small jets that squirt nitrogen gas. The flight controls are located on the ends of the MMU's armrests. A knob on the right arm controls the orientation— up or down, left or right, or turn around. The knob on the left controls the motion forward or backward.

The first time man had ever separated from an orbiting spacecraft with an MMU took place during *Challenger*'s flight in February, 1984, (STS-11). The astronauts were Mission Specialists Bruce Mc-Candless and Robert L. Stewart. Their exciting space walks took place during the fifth day in orbit.

Together, the astronauts moved away from *Challenger* to distances as far as 320 feet, and performed prearranged checkouts of the MMU systems. They also removed a television camera from the cargo bay, for inflight maintenance within the cabin, and later reinstalled it during a second EVA.

A few problems were reported and corrected. One astronaut had trouble locking himself in various foot restraints. Both found they had to yell into the VOX (voice-operated) microphone.

Bruce McCandless, wearing MMU, tries out maximum distance venture during Mission 41-B.

On the second EVA, the following day, the crew performed MMU docking operations in the cargo bay with a payload called SPAS (Shuttle Pallet Satellite). It was to have been deployed, but the Remote Manipulator Arm had a "sore wrist." (SPAS-01 was successfully deployed later.)

The astronauts in the MMUs also retrieved a foot restraint that had come loose, reinstalled the TV camera they had removed for repair, and fixed a slide wire linkage that had come loose. The slide wire is a restraining device for use when wearing only a space suit, without an MMU.

Successful flights with the MMUs are one more step toward eventual assembly of a Space Station. Astronauts in MMUs will move huge sections of the Space Station from the Orbiter's cargo bay and join them together. Later, MMUs will be used for any needed maintenance or repair work.

Left: Astronaut Bruce McCandless rides Remote Manipulator Arm during checkout of Shuttle Pallet Satellite in *Challenger's* cargo bay.

Right: McCandless returns to *Challenger* cargo bay after ride into space wearing MMU.

CHAPTER 6

A Service Call in Space

When you blow a fuse in your TV set, you call a serviceman. He comes to your home, replaces the fuse, and everything works fine. But in space, repairing a faulty satellite is not that simple.

The first satellite repair job was dramatic. Things didn't go as expected. But it all ended up all right. The spacecraft that needed fixing was the Solar Maximum Mission Satellite, called Solar Max for short.

Astronaut Bruce McCandless checks out the MMU in a space walk before use in capturing and repairing Solar Max.

Solar Max had been launched on Valentine's Day, 1980. It went into orbit 269 miles high, to study ultraviolet and X-ray radiation from the Sun. Giant flares were detected that could seriously affect weather on Earth.

After tracking hundreds of such flares, Solar Max lost its fine pointing control. The $77,000,000 satellite was virtually useless. With Space Shuttles now available, NASA knew what had to be done.

On April 8, 1984, Space Shuttle *Challenger* pulled alongside Solar Max. Astronaut George M. Nelson left the Orbiter in his Manned Maneuvering Unit

(MMU) and approached the satellite. He carried a trunion pin device, to lock onto the satellite and bring it back to the cargo bay.

But something went wrong. Solar Max started tumbling. Mission Commander Robert L. Crippen spoke to Nelson: "It looks like you may have bumped it a little bit."

The grappling device had not worked, and Nelson returned to *Challenger*. Back on Earth, flight directors at Goddard Space Flight Center got into the act. They sent signals to Solar Max that managed to stabilize it again.

On April 10, Crippen again carefully maneuvered the Space Shuttle in close to Solar Max. Astronaut Terry Hart, at the controls of the mechanical Manipulator Arm, reached out and grabbed it, then drew it into the cargo bay.

The next day Astronauts James D. van Hoften and Nelson spent more than seven hours repairing Solar Max, one of the longest EVAs on record. Then the mechanical arm lifted Solar Max outside and

Left: Repair mission begins as Mission Specialist George Nelson approaches Solar Max slowly, in orbit 300 miles above Earth.

Right: After failure of EVA attempt to capture Solar Max, *Challenger* moved in and grabbed it with Remote Manipulator Arm.

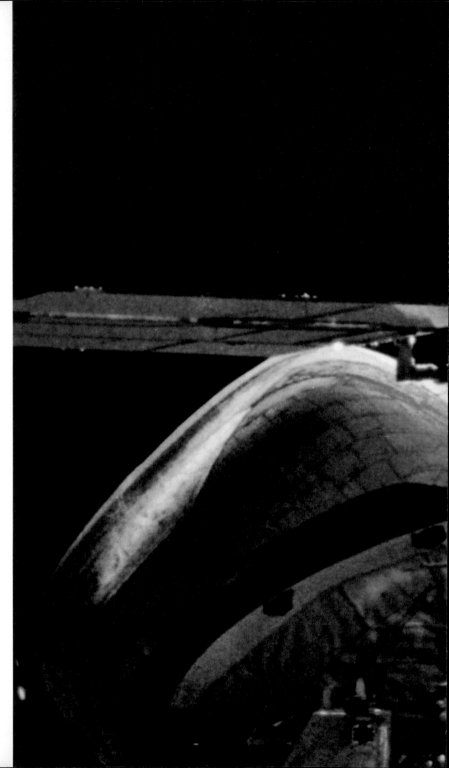

released it into orbit once more. NASA estimated it would have cost $200,000,000 to replace Solar Max with another satellite launch.

With Solar Max back in operation, it is hoped that it will be able to photograph Halley's Comet in 1986 when the comet comes close enough to the Sun for observation.

The remarkable service call in space that repaired Solar Max means that future satellites may no longer have to rely on expensive backup components built into their systems to prevent failure. Other orbiting satellite observatories can have replaceable modules that can be put in place by Space Shuttle repairmen.

Astronauts George Nelson, right, and James van Hoften use Remote Manipulator Arm to work on Solar Max in cargo bay of *Challenger.*

CHAPTER 7

The Space Telescope

Scheduled to be launched from a Space Shuttle in 1985 is the amazing Space Telescope, designed to operate until at least the end of this century. Like Solar Max, it can be retrieved in orbit for any minor repairs to be made in the Shuttle's cargo bay. More advanced equipment can also be installed while it is in space, or it can be returned to Earth for a major overhaul.

The Space Telescope will have a clear view of the heavens, from an altitude of from 310 to 373 miles. Earth-bound telescopes are severely handicapped by having to peer through the atmosphere at distant planets and stars. The Space Telescope will be above the disturbing ocean of air that surrounds our planet. Its images are flashed to Earth electronically, and there converted into sharp pictures.

It will be able to view objects 50 times dimmer than anything ever seen with telescopes on Earth. Astronomers will have a much better look at our own solar system, as well as into deep space. They

How Space Telescope will work in space. Images are sent to Tracking and Data Relay Satellite, then to Earth at rate of 1,000,000 bits per second.

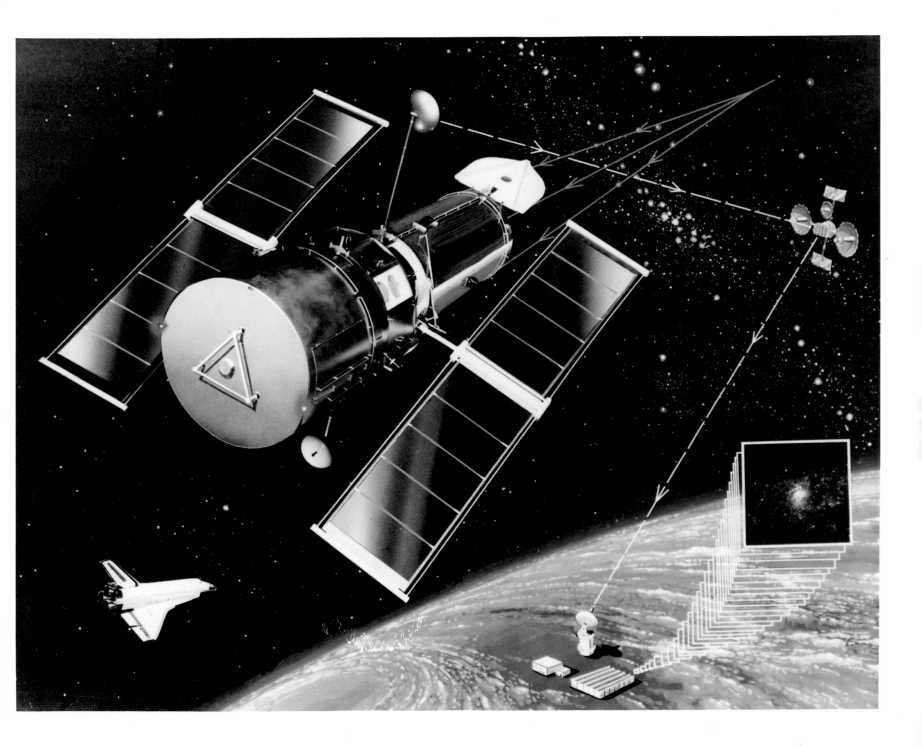

can get closer looks at the clouds of Venus, the ice caps and deep valleys of Mars, and the strange atmosphere and moons of Jupiter.

The Space Telescope will be used to search for

The Space Telescope's 94-inch primary mirror is checked by optical engineers for correct curvature.

possible planets orbiting nearby stars. It will examine quasars, pulsars, and black holes. By seeing farther then ever before, it will give us a better idea of what the universe is like, and perhaps knowledge of the beginning of it all.

This orbiting observatory is 43 ½ feet long, with a diameter of 14 feet. Once it is launched from a Shuttle with the Remote Manipulator Arm, two large solar panels will open out to supply it with electrical power. The primary mirror of the reflecting telescope is 94 inches in diameter. It weighs nearly a ton. There is a smaller secondary mirror. Selection of targets and pointing are controlled from the ground.

Approved by Congress in 1977, the Space Telescope is a marvel of design and engineering. Once in orbit, it will revolutionize our concept of the universe. It will help us to peer back in time and perhaps discover how and when the universe was created. Such knowledge may help us understand what the future holds for us.

Space Telescope will study solar flares like this one pictured by telescope aboard Skylab spacecraft.

CHAPTER 8

"We Deliver"

Hauling cargo into Earth orbits is the real business of the Space Transportation System. So, after the first operational Shuttle flight by *Columbia* on the STS-5 mission, the crew adopted as a motto: WE DELIVER!

On November 11, 1982, during its first day in orbit, *Columbia* successfully deployed the first commercial payload ever carried into orbit aboard a Shuttle—the Satellite Business Systems 3 (SBS-C). The next day it deployed ANIK-C, a satellite of the Canadian TELESAT Corporation.

Hundreds more satellites will be launched from Space Shuttles before the end of this century. Some will send back pictures and information of distant galaxies and other mysteries of deep space. Others will improve international communications and television reception. Still more will provide better weather forecasts and help us manage our limited natural resources and Earth's threatened environment.

In April, 1984, the Space Shuttle *Challenger* carried into orbit a huge unmanned scientific satellite called the Long Duration Exposure Facility. Nearly the size of a city bus, LDEF carried 57 experiments housed in shallow trays. Many of them were to learn how living organisms and man-made materials can stand up in space over a period of time.

Challenger launches Long Duration Exposure Facility, un-manned satellite carrying 57 scientific payloads, including 12,000,000 tomato seeds for student project.

This information is needed to know how space colonists of the future can live safely under constant bombardment of cosmic rays and other radiation in space. Samples of materials that will be used to construct space stations were on board. Such materials are now widely used in building aircraft.

We also need to know how plants grow in space and what happens to seeds exposed to zero gravity. One experiment aboard the first LDEF flight was called SEEDS (Space Exposed Experiment Developed for Students). Some 12,000,000 tiny tomato seeds were packaged in dacron bags and sealed in aluminum canisters. The same number of seeds was stored on Earth for comparison.

LDEF was scheduled to be recovered from orbit after 18 months in space and returned to Earth. Then the seeds would be divided up into laboratory kits for educational study in schools. Each kit would contain 50 seeds from the LDEF and 50 seeds from the Earth storage group. Tomato seeds were chosen because they are small, and are familiar to all areas of the United Sates. Besides, they are easy to germinate and grow.

The kits are to be distributed in the fall of 1985. Students receiving them will be asked to report the results of their individual investigations back to NASA. The program allows students to take part in space study by becoming involved in actual experiments.

On an earlier flight, *Challenger* released the Shuttle Pallet Satellite (SPAS-01) with the Remote Manipulator Arm to photograph the Orbiter itself. Remarkable pictures were taken by remote camera aboard SPAS-01 from 1,000 feet away over the Atlantic Ocean.

Space Shuttles will carry to and from orbit many different kinds of satellites during the years ahead. They will provide information that will make life far better on Earth. Satellites are useful for all sorts of things, such as mapping the Earth, improving communications, providing search-and-rescue information, detecting possible earthquake zones.

Remarkable photograph of Orbiter *Challenger* taken by remote camera aboard SPAS-01 from 1,000 feet away, over Atlantic Ocean.

CHAPTER 9

Space Stations

On January 25, 1984, President Ronald Reagan directed the National Aeronautics and Space Administration "to develop a permanently manned Space Station, and to do it within a decade."

The future Space Station has been described as "a human-built island in orbit on which men and women can live and work as long as they want."

NASA design engineers describe it as a habitat "to be fully equipped for six to eight engineers, scientists, technicians, and other specialists." Their places will be taken, before they return to Earth after a few months in orbit, by others who will continue their work. Thus, the Space Station will be continuously inhabited.

Scheduled to go into operation in the 1990s, the Space Station will be built from modules prefabricated on Earth. These will then be transported to orbit in a Space Shuttle's cargo bay. They will be unloaded and assembled by astronauts wearing space suits and propelled by jet-powered MMU backpacks.

Space Shuttle docks with future Space Station. Space voyagers will live and work in shirt-sleeve environment inside the cylinders.

Space Shuttles will bring up components of future Space Stations. Astronauts, wearing MMUs, will assemble them.

connecting passageway, become the command control center, living quarters, and laboratory. The service modules are positioned below the cylinders. They will hold the life-support systems, power unit, communications apparatus, an airlock, and a docking berth for the arriving and departing Space Shuttle Orbiter.

Inside the modules crews will live and work in a shirt-sleeve environment, just as at home on Earth. Outside the modules will be attached pallets and remotely controlled experiments and observation instruments. Other instruments will be aboard free-flying platforms in nearby orbits.

The crew will conduct basic research in medicine, astronomy, space physics, and solar studies, as well as Earth science studies and technology experiments to learn how to manufacture products in zero gravity. The Space Station will become a national laboratory.

Among the first payloads would be two giant cylinders and some service units that would be lifted from the Shuttle by its "space crane" Manipulator Arm and plugged together. The cylinders, with a

NASA's Concept B Space Station looks like a giant wagon wheel. Space colonists will live inside the hollow circular tube. It will turn slowly to create artificial gravity.

Costing more than $8 billion, the Space Station is designed for expansion, by adding more modules if larger crews and more equipment are needed. It is called a "modular building block" design.

Like a giant Erector set, antenna frameworks will be built in orbit to supply power for Space Stations where products will be manufactured in zero gravity.

Huge panels like giant paddlewheels covered with solar cells will provide electrical energy. Other panels will hold radiators to release heat from the Space Station.

By the time the Space Station is ready for assembly, Space Shuttles are planned to land regularly at Kennedy Space Center in Florida. Earlier Shuttle flights have landed primarily at Edwards Air Force Base in California, but the Orbiter then has to be piggybacked across the country, which is costly and time-consuming. Other landings have been made at White Sands, New Mexico. Emergency landings can also be made at several other runways around the world.

The Space Station, like the Space Shuttles, is expected to become profitable in the future. It will be vital to future commercial space operations of all kinds. It will provide a continuing place to work in orbit. It will permit crews to make routine maintenance and repairs of other space equipment.

Future planetary space flights could be launched

NASA's concept for a Solar Space Base Platform. Scientists and other researchers will live in circular tube that rotates to make artificial gravity.

from the Space Station much more easily and less expensively than launching from Earth. There would be no energy-wasting climb through the dense atmosphere to start their long journeys.

Just as Spacelab was the creation of the European Space Agency, so will the first Space Station be international. The ESA and individual nations such as Canada and Japan already are joining in studies of how they can use its facilities when they are ready.

As has been pointed out, "The 20th Century, which began with history's first successful flight of a power-driven aircraft at Kitty Hawk, North Carolina, will very likely end with the first truly permanent, orbital, human habitat firmly emplaced in space."

The time will come when people on Earth will be dependent on Space Stations and the advances made in the use of zero gravity. Young people, reading this book, may want to think of careers in science and technology so that they will be able to seek positions aboard a Space Station.

Summary of Early Shuttle Flights

STS-1—April 12-14, 1981. *Columbia* flew 36 orbits, covered 1,074,567 miles in orbit at 166 miles, in 54 hours, 21 minutes, 57 seconds. Landed at Edwards AFB, California. Commander: John W. Young. Pilot: Robert L. Crippen. All major objectives accomplished.

STS-2—November 12-14, 1981. *Columbia* flew 36 orbits, covered 1,074,567 miles in orbit at 157 miles, in 54 hours, 24 minutes, 4 seconds. Landed at Edwards AFB, California. Commander: Joe Engle. Pilot: Richard Truly. Ninety percent of major objectives accomplished.

STS-3—March 22-30, 1982. *Columbia* flew 130 orbits, covered 4,400,000 miles in orbit at 147 miles, in 8 days, 6 minutes, 9 seconds. Landed at White Sands Missile Range, New Mexico. Commander: Jack Lousma. Pilot: C. Gordon Fullerton. Ninety percent of major objectives accomplished.

STS-4—June 27-July 4, 1982. *Columbia* flew 112 orbits, covered 3,300,000 miles in orbit at 197 miles in 7 days, 1 hour, 10 minutes, 43 seconds. Landed at Edwards AFB. Commander: Thomas K. Mattingly. Pilot: Henry Hartsfield, Jr. Two winning entries in NASA's Shuttle Student Involvement Project were aboard.

STS-5—November 11-16, 1982. *Columbia* flew 81 orbits, covered 1,800,000 miles in orbit at 184 miles, in 5 days, 2 hours, 15 minutes, 29 seconds. Landed at Edwards AFB. Commander: Vance D. Brand. Pilot: Robert F. Overmyer. Mission Specialists: William Lenoir, Joseph Allen. First operational Shuttle mission. Fifty-three of 55 objectives accomplished. Two satellites launched in orbit—SBS-C and ANIK-C.

STS-6—April 4-9, 1983. *Challenger* flew 80 orbits, covered 2,092,838 miles in orbit at 176.6 miles, in 5 days, 24 minutes,

31 seconds. Landed at Edwards AFB. Commander: Paul Weitz. Pilot: Karol Bobko. Deployed Tracking Data Relay Satellite (TDRS-A) into orbit. Mission Specialists Donald Peterson and F. Story Musgrave performed EVA activity in cargo bay wearing Extra-Vehicular Mobility Units (EMUs).

STS-7—June 18-24, 1983. *Challenger* flew 97 orbits, covered 2,530,567 miles in orbit at 184 miles, in 6 days, 2 hours, 25 minutes, 41 seconds. Landed at Edwards AFB. Commander: Robert L. Crippen. Pilot: Frederick H. Hauck. Mission Specialists: Sally K. Ride, Norman E. Thagard, John M. Fabian. Fifty-six of 58 objectives accomplished. Deployed two communications satellites—Canadian TELESAT and Indonesian PALAPA. Shuttle Pallet Satellite released with Remote Manipulator System and photographed *Challenger* in flight.

STS-8—August 30-September 5, 1983. *Challenger* flew 97 orbits, covered 2,514,478 miles in orbit at 184 miles, in 6 days, 1 hour, 9 minutes, 32 seconds. Landed at Edwards AFB in first night landing. Commander: Richard H. Truly. Pilot: Daniel C. Brandenstein. Mission Specialists: Guion S. Bluford, Jr., Dale A. Gardner, William E. Thornton. Major objectives accomplished. Deployed INSAT-1B satellite.

STS-9—November 28-December 8, 1983. *Columbia* flew 166 orbits, covered 4,295,853 miles in orbit at 155 miles, in 10 days, 7 hours, 48 minutes, 17 seconds. Landed at Edwards AFB. Commander: John W. Young. Pilot: Brewster Shaw. Mission Specialists: Robert Parker, Owen Garriott. Payload Specialists: Byron K. Lichtenberg, Ulf Merbold. Primary objective—Verification Flight Tests (VFTs) of Spacelab—accomplished.

Mission 41-B—February 3-11, 1984. *Challenger* flew 127 orbits, varying from 174 to 202 miles, in 7 days, 23 hours, 17 minutes. Landed at Kennedy Space Center, Florida. Commander: Vance Brand. Pilot: Robert Gibson. Mission Specialists: Bruce McCandless, Robert Stewart, Ronald McNair. Primary objectives accomplished. Deployed two communications satellites—Westar VI and Indonesian PALAPA-B2. Evaluation of Manned Maneuvering Unit (MMU).

Mission 41-C—April 6-13, 1984. *Challenger* flew 107 orbits, averaging 309 miles in altitude, in 6 days, 22 hours, 38 minutes, 55 seconds. Landed at Edwards AFB. Commander: Robert L. Crippen. Pilot: Frances Scobee. Mission Specialists: Terry Hart, James D. van Hoften, George M. Nelson. All 25 objectives accomplished, including launch of LDEF and repair of Solar Max satellite.

Mission 41-D—August 30-September 5, 1984. *Discovery* flew 96 orbits at 184 miles in altitude, in 6 days, 56 minutes, 4 seconds. Landed at Edwards AFB. Commander: Henry W. Hartsfield, Jr. Pilot: Michael L. Coats. Mission Specialists: Steven A. Hawley, Judith A. Resnik, Richard M. Mullane. Payload Specialist: Charles D. Walker. Successfully deployed three satellites, tested 102-foot-tall solar energy panel, and removed ice on outside of Orbiter with the Remote Manipulator Arm.

Glossary

ABORT—To end a mission short of its goal, for emergency or malfunction.

AIRLOCK—A chamber used to adjust pressure when passing from cabin area to space environment.

APOLLO—Three-man U.S. spacecraft; used for Moon flights.

BLACKOUT—Loss of radio signals during atmosphere re-entry.

CARGO BAY—Area of Space Shuttle where payloads are carried. Open to space, pressurized space suits are required for working there.

DEORBIT BURN—Firing of a retrorocket to slow spacecraft for atmosphere re-entry.

DOCK—To join two spacecraft together in orbit.

EVA—Extra-Vehicular Activity outside spacecraft, using space suit.

EXTERNAL FUEL TANK—Holds fuel for Orbiter's engines; only part of Space Shuttle not reusable.

FUEL CELL—Device for mixing hydrogen and oxygen to produce electricity and pure water.

G—The force or pull of Earth's gravity on your body at sea level.

GEMINI—Second manned U.S. spacecraft, two-place.

HANDHOLD—Portable device with suction cups; used to keep body steady while in weightlessness.

MERCURY—First manned U.S. spacecraft, one-place.

MID-DECK—Living area in a Space Shuttle with accommodations for eating, sleeping, hygiene, waste disposal.

MMU—Manned Maneuvering Unit attached to space suit for movement outside spacecraft.

NASA—National Aeronautics and Space Administration.

ORBIT—Path flown by spacecraft where its tendency to fly off into space is balanced by Earth's gravity.

ORBITER—Main part of Space Shuttle; goes into orbit.

PAYLOAD—The useful cargo, such as experiments or satellites, that a Space Shuttle carries.

RMS—Remote Manipulator System with mechanical arm which moves objects in and out of the cargo bay in space.

SHIRT-SLEEVE ENVIRONMENT—Area where pressurized space suit is not needed.

SKYLAB—Early U.S. orbiting laboratory, now disintegrated.

SOLAR CELL—Device that produces electricity when struck by sunlight.

SOLID ROCKET BOOSTERS—The two reusable solid fuel rockets that provide most of the power to launch a Space Shuttle.

SPACE SHUTTLE—First reusable U.S. aerospace craft.

SPACELAB—Advanced space laboratory flown in cargo bay of Space Shuttles.

STS—Space Transportation System.

WEIGHTLESSNESS—Condition of zero gravity in orbit.

Index